SYSTEMATIC SUCCESSION PLANNING
Building Leadership from Within

Rebecca Luhn Wolfe, Ph.D.

A FIFTY-MINUTE™ SERIES BOOK

CRISP PUBLICATIONS, INC.
Menlo Park, California

SYSTEMATIC SUCCESSION PLANNING
Building Leadership from Within

Rebecca Luhn Wolfe, Ph.D.

CREDITS
Managing Editor: **Kathleen Barcos**
Editor: **Kay Keppler**
Typesetting: **ExecuStaff**
Cover Design: **Carol Harris**
Artwork: **Ralph Mapson**

Copyright © 1996 by Crisp Publications, Inc.

Printed in the United States of America by Bawden Printing Company.

Distribution to the U.S. Trade:

National Book Network, Inc.
4720 Boston Way
Lanham, MD 20706
1-800-462-6420

Library of Congress Catalog Card Number 95-83113
Wolfe, Rebecca Luhn
Systematic Succession Planning
ISBN 1-56052-380-8

This book is printed on recyclable paper with soy ink.

LEARNING OBJECTIVES FOR:

SYSTEMATIC SUCCESSION PLANNING

The objectives for *Systematic Succession Planning* are listed below. They have been developed to guide you, the reader, to the core issues covered in this book.

Objectives

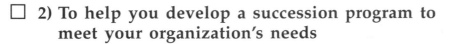

- ☐ 1) **To explain the benefits of a systematic succession plan**

- ☐ 2) **To help you develop a succession program to meet your organization's needs**

- ☐ 3) **To show how to identify leaders and leadership positions.**

- ☐ 4) **To explain the operation and evaluation of a systematic succession plan**

Assessing Your Progress

In addition to the Learning Objectives, *Systematic Succession Planning* includes a unique new **assessment tool*** which can be found at the back of this book. A twenty-five item, multiple choice/true-false questionnaire allows the reader to evaluate his or her comprehension of the subject matter covered. An answer sheet, with a chart matching the questions to the listed objectives, is also provided.

* Assessments should not be used in any selection process.

ABOUT THE AUTHOR

Rebecca Luhn Wolfe, Ph.D., is president of Innovative Consulting Services, a Houston-based training firm. She has been involved in corporate business education for several years, including positions held as director of training for a large health care management firm and for a major airline. Dr. Luhn's interest in business and professional development has resulted in the publication of three other books, *Buying Your First Franchise, Managing Anger,* and *Employee Benefits with Cost Control* by Crisp Publications, Inc. and academic works on file in many universities. Dr. Luhn earned a Ph.D. in Business Communications and also holds the Distinguished Americans award for her contributions to education. She often lectures at Rice University and the University of Houston.

In addition to writing, her focus is providing consulting services with a range of expertise in business for both small and large corporations.

ABOUT THE SERIES

With over 200 titles in print, the acclaimed Crisp 50-Minute™ series presents self-paced learning at its easiest and best. These comprehensive self-study books for business or personal use are filled with exercises, activities, assessments, and case studies that capture your interest and increase your understanding.

Other Crisp products, based on the 50-Minute books, are available in a variety of learning style formats for both individual and group study, including audio, video, CD-ROM, and computer-based training.

Dedication

To my husband, Myron, the greatest leader I've ever known. Where you go I will follow.

CONTENTS

CONTENTS (continued)

SECTION

1

Succession Planning: An Overview

> **“**_Let our advance worrying become advance thinking and planning._**”**
>
> —Winston Churchill

THE TRUE MEANING OF SUCCESSION PLANNING

Most of us have an idea about what succession planning means to an organization, but few companies have a formal and effective succession planning program in place. The need is great for a company to plan for those who will be future leaders. Temporary and permanent backup talent also should be established.

What is *true* succession planning? If it were just the textbook definition: "the systematic steps or design that allows for one to follow another in time or place," it would be simple. However, using the simplest definition, our top positions could be filled by those who are not prepared for the challenge or who do not want the responsibility. Companies want and need more from their succession plan. They

- need the excellent performance in their company preserved.

- need important leadership positions identified.

- want to strengthen individual advancement.

- want to have the right leaders prepared for the right positions at the needed time.

THE TRUE MEANING OF SUCCESSION PLANNING (continued)

Thus, the true meaning of succession planning is:

"A defined program that an organization systemizes to ensure leadership continuity for all key positions by developing activities that will build personnel talent from within."

> ### PRESENT TALENT = FUTURE TALENT

Recognizing Key People

Many focus on management positions when they think of succession planning. Our focus is on all positions. A solid plan begins with reviewing which positions are really necessary in the company. Key people are found in almost all job positions—including executives, sales, marketing, technical, clerical, and processing personnel. Continuation of talent is no longer limited to the CEO or top management. It should involve all who make a defined and necessary contribution to the organization.

JUST-IN-CASE STUDIES: WHAT WOULD YOUR COMPANY DO?

#1: A Doubtful Choice

Your CEO is one year away from retirement. For several years management has expected Tim to be his replacement. Tim's experience is unmatched, and his performance had been excellent.

As the clock ticks down for Tim to become the new CEO, the board of directors has discovered some unsettling news about him. Investigated rumors about Tim's compulsive gambling have been confirmed. A broken marriage, lost real estate, and depression were uncovered as part of Tim's hidden burdens.

The CEO has a great deal invested in Tim, but how can he allow someone with this type of personal irresponsibility to assume a top position in the corporation? The board and the CEO know that no one else within the company is groomed for this responsibility, and they wonder how effective an outside search will be on such short notice.

#2: Talent Lost

You are the CEO of an advertising and public relations agency. Your company jet crashed with your top personnel on board. No one survived. These people were not only the best in your company, they were the best in the business. Your biggest accounts are now hesitant to commit to any future projects. Your executive v.p. of sales turns to you and asks, "Now what?"

JUST-IN-CASE STUDIES: WHAT WOULD YOUR COMPANY DO? (continued)

#3: No Trained Back-up

You've flown in 80 sales reps from all divisional offices across the United States for the kick-off of a new product. The national marketing director, Jim, plans on making this introduction in a two-day seminar at a luxury resort, which cost thousands to organize. On the first day of the presentation, Jim develops severe laryngitis. His assistant is not prepared for such an intense seminar. Jim has no other trained back-up.

#4: Moving On

One Monday morning Janice, your systems analyst, comes to you with her regrets that after 10 years in her position she is leaving the company for another job with less pay but more supervisory responsibility. You explain that she had never been offered that type of position in your company because you didn't know she had the interest, and you felt she never had acquired "people skills." Janice wondered how she could have acquired those skills staying in the same position for 10 years.

* * *

As you can see from these fictional but possible case studies, a company of any size should have a formal succession planning program. You will learn later how these companies could have solved their problems. An effective solution is possible, but until you know your succession planning options, you can't develop an effective plan.

Employees at every level are the greatest asset a company can have. To survive the world of business, we must protect our employees, for they are our future leaders.

THE IMPORTANCE OF A SOLID PLAN

A succession plan can establish a strategy for existing resources and personnel, justify new resources, make it easier to contend with corporate changes, and present alternatives in a new environment. It also:

- Provides direction for corporate long-range planning, ensuring the best use of resources to achieve growth and profitability

- Defines goals and missions and prepares individuals for achievement

- Provides development programs to ensure growth and continuity

- Helps assess corporate functions and results

Many companies have cited leadership succession as one of their top priorities. Read the following list and check your top three priorities.

☐ Chance is not a good means by which to conduct any business.

☑ Having the right people in the right jobs can keep a company on top in a competitive market.

☑ Strategic planning includes strategic leadership.

☑ Individual development creates a positive environment.

☐ Leadership succession sets training and other developmental programs on a clear path.

☐ Leadership succession establishes direction and consistent goals for individuals.

☐ Leadership succession enhances communications.

☐ Leadership succession creates challenging and measurable performance objectives.

These are not the only reasons for an organization to formulate a succession planning program. Let's examine some of these important reasons and other considerations.

REASONS FOR A SUCCESSION PLAN

#1. Identifying Highly Talented Individuals

Many people in every company have exceptional talent and performance, and every company should identify and advance these workers. A succession plan offers a way to do this.

#2. Promoting Employee Development

Many employees are hired knowing that they will require continuing training to meet the needs of their job. Others require additional education to advance and individual attention is often provided for those identified for rapid advancement in the corporation. Succession planning justifies the high cost of training and time devoted to employee development. Identifying future replacement needs requires a systematic plan and a solid development program.

#3. Refining Corporate Planning

Successful companies always have a long-range, formal plan that covers all business operations. Planning is a continuous and systematic process that prepares a company for the future.

Most plans begin with a mission statement that identifies the organization's fundamental purpose. The mission is followed by the company objectives and goals along with actions or strategies. Part of the strategies are human resource needs and activities, including succession planning.

#4. Establishing the Talent Pool

Companies realize that last-minute replacement of key individuals does not work. Establishing a talent pool of gifted employees to fill positions is not only wise, but often a must. For some companies, "pool" may mean several individuals; for others, it may represent one targeted successor.

HOW RESTRUCTURING AFFECTS SUCCESSION PLANNING

In times of recession, many companies merge with other companies or move overseas to enhance profits. This often results in layoffs and reorganizations for domestic workers. Millions of jobs have been cut from all sizes of companies, but much of the work still needs to be done. These responsibilities are allocated to those most capable of performing the tasks, and succession planning is an excellent tool to identify how and to whom the work should be reallocated. Such a program can also increase or at least maintain a high standard of quality and production.

Succession planning should be implemented for many reasons, some of which have been discussed. List additional reasons why an SSP program would benefit your organization.

1. Benefit: _____

_____

Why: _____

_____

2. Benefit: _____

_____

Why: _____

_____

3. Benefit: _____

_____

Why: _____

_____

OTHER FACTORS AFFECTING SUCCESSION PLANNING?

Economic forces can affect organizational plans in one way or another. The impact of these may differ by company size, location, stability and type of business. Trends that affect companies the most are additional workload requirements, diversification of workers, technology, fewer resources, competition, the global market and changing views toward employment security. What trends have affected your organization?

_____

_____

_____

_____

The Common Problem Areas

► **MANAGEMENT SUPPORT**—Top management must support the succession planning program or it will fail

► **PARTICIPATION**—Participation from all divisions and work areas is needed to make it part of corporate policy

► **DOCUMENTATION**—Keeping up with the paperwork and keeping the program uniform and fair requires that it be considered a priority

► **UNDERSTANDING**—It is a systematic program and every phase should be communicated clearly and concisely

► **FOLLOW-UP**—Too few meetings can lead to limited follow-up with the planned action steps

► **PREPARATION**—Thinking for the long term and planning for future needs is necessary

► **THE WRITTEN WORD**—Write it down and distribute it with updates periodically

YOU BE THE JUDGE

Read the following case study and write down the characteristics of the succession planning program at Trymax, Inc. that you think are effective and others you would improve. Compare your list to the checklist following the case study.

CASE STUDY: Trymax, Inc.

Trymax is a traditional company. The CEO was preparing to retire in the next few years and told the vice president of human resources that he was to have replacements in line for him and all senior executives of the company.

The vice president of human resources scheduled appointments with executives and department heads. He researched succession planning by visiting well-established companies and other established organizations in the same business. After benchmarking practices in other organizations, he developed a plan he felt would support an effective program.

With the names of potential successors in hand and a basic plan, he called a meeting of training personnel and asked them to set up a series of activities for leadership development and training seminars geared toward high-potential advancement. Each potential successor was to attend the scheduled events throughout the next year.

The trainers were asked to evaluate the classroom progress of each future leader, and the results were given to their bosses to add to their employee evaluations. The individuals then waited for position vacancies before they could advance their careers.

YOU BE THE JUDGE (continued)

What's Wrong with This Picture?

Trymax is trying to have a succession planning program, but will they have a successful and effective program?

1. What did they do right, if anything?

_____

_____

2. What did they do wrong?

_____

_____

3. Where are the gaps in the steps taken?

_____

_____

4. What is missing from the plan?

_____

_____

5. What would you do to fix the program?

_____

_____

Check the case study and Trymax Succession plan for

☐ Executive participation and personnel support

☐ Focused objectives matched to company objectives

☐ Performance assessment

☐ Future-driven activities

☐ Key job understanding

☐ Defined responsibilities

☐ Identified best practices

☐ Understanding replacement needs

☐ Individual development practices

☐ High potentials identified

☐ Emphasis on results

☐ Sharing information

☐ New challenges for employees

☐ Solid evaluation process

✳   ✳   ✳

Now that you have an idea of how involved a succession plan must be and how easy it is to miss valuable steps toward an effective plan, we will look at the process from start to finish.

SETTING THE STAGE

Fear and uncertainty can make people resist change. For every new direction an organization takes, excellent communication and commitment and sound, unbiased judgment are needed. Laying the foundation for a succession planning program can be a major effort. The following six steps show how the system works and how succession planning fits into the big picture.

STEP 1

DEFINE YOUR MISSION

Should detail your corporate mission statement and the purpose of the succession plan

STEP 2

CONSTRUCT ASSESSMENTS

Should detail internal and external issues, including information about your environment, resources and potential

STEP 3

IDENTIFY STRATEGIC ISSUES

Should state any areas of tension and the most important opportunities and problems

STEP 4

SET OBJECTIVES AND GOALS

Should define purpose and results

STEP 5

DEVELOP STRATEGIC ACTION

Should outline action steps taken to achieve the organizational and succession objectives

STEP 6

ESTABLISH PROGRAMS

Should describe plans and activities that will be used to carry out the strategies and provide the resources necessary for success

CHOOSING YOUR APPROACH

Before beginning any planning process, know what will be your plan of action. No one approach is best, and what works well for one company may not work for another. Review the following approaches and assess which would best match your company's business. You may choose as many as necessary.

☐ **CAREER-DRIVEN APPROACH:** Planning careers to match corporate goals

☐ **COMPETITIVE MARKET APPROACH:** Maintaining a competitive edge in the market with talent that will stay on top of the situation

☐ **VISIONARY APPROACH:** Anticipating the future and planning the leadership talent around those needs

☐ **PROBLEM-SOLVING APPROACH:** Solving problems that confront the company

☐ **CORPORATE-DIRECTED APPROACH:** Corporate strategizing includes the visions and values of top executives

SUCCESSION PLANNING VERSUS REPLACEMENT PLANNING

As a company charts its course toward leadership continuity, it must be careful not to confuse simple replacement planning with the systematic direction of a solid succession plan. The main differences are:

COMPARISON	
Replacement Planning Mode	**Succession Planning Mode**
Reactive	Pro-Active
Form of Risk Management	Planned Future Development
Substituting	Renewing
Narrow Approach	Organized Alignment
Restricted	Flexible

Replacement planning mode focuses on risk management and ideals for coping with crisis. Succession planning mode works toward continued leadership and talent building so that an organization can continue with planned wisdom and foresight. The two activities often overlap and always compliment each other.

Replacement Planning?   Succession Planning?

SECTION

2

Establishing a Need for Succession Planning

"The time to repair the roof is when the sun is shining."

—John F. Kennedy

PRESENTING A CASE FOR CHANGE

Change is the only constant in business. Any changing organization faces opposition, and this resistance can stifle positive action.

For a company that has never had a formal or informal succession plan, trying to implement one can be a major effort if a solid case for change is not presented to the decision makers. Top management will need to support the plan if such a program is to be established.

How Is This Done?

- Assess current practices and related problems

- Establish a valid need and concrete benefits

- Connect the corporate strategy with succession planning strategies.

- Use benchmarking

- Develop a rough draft of the proposed plan

- List guidelines to consider

- Gain consensus and commitment

By starting with this list you can create your program. You will lay the foundation for change, making it easier to build a solid system for leadership continuity.

UNCOVERING PROBLEMS

Information about past and present problems as they relate to finding talent and qualified leadership will establish a need for solutions. Here are a few problems that could be uncovered.

- Employees charge that advancement is made on a personal, subjective basis rather than an objective criteria of who is best qualified for the position.

- Key positions take too long to fill and, as a result, production suffers.

- People are trained after they are promoted.

- Turnover in priority positions is high.

- Staff complains that the new replacement is not getting the job done.

- High-talent employees are recruited out of the organization.

Succession planning in some companies can be so informal that communications can completely break down. Few may have a good feel for the way replacements are handled, and filling leadership positions turns into a crisis. If the present system works for the most part, document the process to formulate a more systematic plan. You will need an interviewing system, a written survey, and informal meetings to discuss status. Some of the questions you need to ask top managers include:

1. How is leadership continuity handled at all levels?

_____

_____

_____

2. What ideas can be explored for organizing a succession planning program?

_____

_____

_____

3. What are the key positions in their areas?

_____

_____

_____

4. How would they be replaced if they left their key positions?

_____

_____

_____

5. What positions are critical to the continued success of the company?

_____

_____

_____

6. How many key position losses have they experienced from their areas over their tenure with the company?

_____

_____

_____

7. How can talent and future leaders in their departments or divisions be identified?

_____

_____

_____

UNCOVERING PROBLEMS (continued)

8. How can these individuals be developed?

_____

_____

_____

9. Are their employees motivated and do they have an opportunity for advancement?

_____

_____

_____

10. Would they promote from within or go to an outside source to fill a vacant position?

_____

_____

_____

Formulate Your Questions

Knowing only as much as you know now, would you change how you replace key personnel? What questions would you ask top management and executive officers in your corporation?

1. _____

2. _____

3. _____

DEFINING YOUR NEEDS

Before taking your proposal to the decision makers, you'll need to illustrate how succession planning benefits the organization. Remember that in any new proposal you must answer the question "Why should we support this?" long before it is asked.

1st   Show your findings and outline the critical issues in managing succession from past years.

2nd   Describe how future alternatives and possibilities in strategic planning will affect the future of the company and employees.

3rd   Explain actions that can influence results.

4th   Describe expenses connected to operating a systematic succession planning program.

CONNECTING THE STRATEGIES

One plan does not fit all. Organizations have different requirements for their succession planning programs. Your design will be based on how large your company is, the type of business, how long in business, expertise available, and other factors that must be considered before any design can be developed. Top-priority considerations are the goals of officers and executives, the strategic objectives of the organization, and human resource objectives.

EXERCISE:
Ask Yourself

Before continuing with "Your Case for Change," ask yourself:

	Yes	No
Are decision makers willing to change their replacement procedure radically?	☐	☐
Are decision makes willing to commit to fill key positions from within the organization and plan for alternatives when necessary?	☐	☐
Are decision makers ready to commit their resources to developing leadership talent?	☐	☐
Is the present organizational plan solid?	☐	☐
Are decision makers willing to give the time required to follow through with a succession planning program?	☐	☐
Are top managers familiar with a formal succession planning program?	☐	☐

Defining Strategy

Corporate strategy describes a firm's primary performance objectives, major operating procedures, and product-market scope. Primary objectives state the criteria by which management measures the success of the firm and presumes that this is how others will measure it. Product-market scope sets the environmental boundaries for operating, followed by operating policies that specify how a company conducts its activities. When reviewing your company's business policy, look at how managers define, form, implement, and manage the corporate objectives.

Succession plans must be linked to human resource objectives. Assessing how your human resource department functions, its goals and strategies, will help your foundation for a strategic succession plan. Human resource practices should show a solid link to corporate practices. This evidence will support your effort. The things you will need to know are as follows.

- Goals and objectives of your human resource department

- How HR has contributed formally to leadership continuity

- Type of support present in HR

- How much HR is involved in corporate strategy

- Practices for developing key employees

- What priority training is given

- Labor relations agreements now in force

Compare human resources practices to the proposed succession planning needs and demonstrate how this encourages or discourages leadership continuity.

EXERCISE:
Preparing Your Proposal

List the questions you'll ask to prepare your succession planning proposal as it relates to both corporate and human resource strategy. Here are a few hints for getting your questionnaire started. Gear your questions toward your organization. Make your notes in the space provided after each question. You'll want to know:

1. How are key positions defined in your company?

_____

2. How are work requirements clarified for each position?

_____

3. What is the view on employee evaluations?

_____

4. How are evaluations conducted?

_____

5. How is exceptional talent documented?

_____

6. Have the requirements for key positions changed in the past few years?

_____

7. What resources are needed to develop leadership in the organization?

_____

8. What are the strengths and weakness of training practices?

_____

9. How can succession planning policy be improved?

_____

10. Is there a formal system for identifying replacement needs from retirement losses?

_____

11. Have layoffs or reorganizations overloaded key talent?

_____

12. Is key talent motivated or disenchanted?

_____

13. What is done when key people depart unexpectedly?

_____

14. Do key people feel that their skills are up to date?

_____

15. Is the organizational structure secure enough to support a strategic succession plan?

_____

FINDING OUT WHERE YOU STAND: BENCHMARKING

Benchmarking is one tool that can move management's interest in your succession plan from low or medium to high. The best companies have exemplary succession planning programs in place, which can persuade decision makers to adopt similar plans.

Benchmarking compares one company's products, services and *practices* against the best competition or those who have been formally recognized as industry leaders. It can clarify successful succession planning programs and serve as a guide for your own department. How do you benchmark?

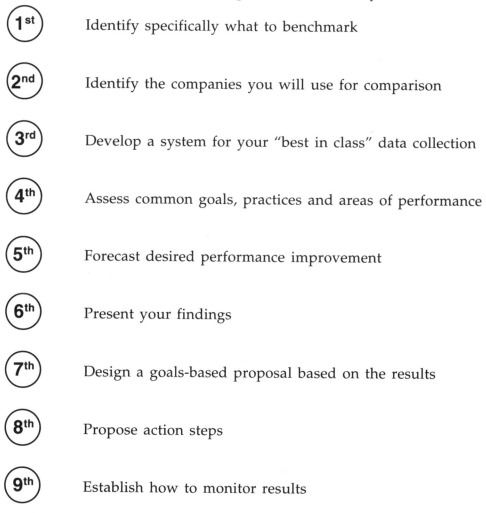

1st	Identify specifically what to benchmark
2nd	Identify the companies you will use for comparison
3rd	Develop a system for your "best in class" data collection
4th	Assess common goals, practices and areas of performance
5th	Forecast desired performance improvement
6th	Present your findings
7th	Design a goals-based proposal based on the results
8th	Propose action steps
9th	Establish how to monitor results
10th	Check your new results against the best again and again

Practices of the Best

Attractive Organizational Environment

+

Rewarding and Challenging Opportunities

+

Identification of High Potentials and Needs

+

Competitively Intense Recruiting

+

Planned Internal and Individual Development

+

Rewards and Recognition

=

Individuals with leadership skills, potential, energy, drive and motivation to meet organizational goals for the present and future

Following you will find Data Collection and a Performance Comparison Worksheet and Summary. Use these as your guides.

DATA COLLECTION

STUDY TOPIC: *Succession Planning*   DATE: _____

SUBJECT MATTER EXPERTS		
Name	**Department**	**Phone**

METHOD:

☐ Interview   ☐ Survey   ☐ Visit   ☐ Other

	Generate Questions	Develop Instrument	Pilot/ Revise	Finalize
Designer/ Developer **Completion Date**				

CONTENTS ANALYSIS

Topic	Data Required	Information Source	Interviewer/ Collector	Due Date/ Complete

COMPARISON WORKSHEET

STUDY TOPIC: PERFORMANCE
(Performance Gap: Difference compared to own performance.)

	OWN COMPANY:	COMPANY A:	COMPANY B:	COMPANY C:
TOPIC:		GAP:	GAP:	GAP:
TOPIC:		GAP:	GAP:	GAP:
TOPIC:		GAP:	GAP:	GAP:
REASONS FOR GAP:				
ADDITIONAL INFORMATION REQUIRED:				

SUMMARY WORKSHEET

PROCESS: _____

Critical Success Factor: _____

Process Owner: _____ Date: _____

SUMMARY OF RESULTS:

OBJECTIVE:

GOALS:

BENCHMARK:

Company: _____

Date Observed: _____

Level: _____ Rate: _____

STRATEGY (OWNER):

TARGETS & MILESTONES:

GETTING COMMITMENT

Without the commitment of the decision maker and all levels of management, your plan will probably fail. Change is never easy, and gaining acceptance to change is even more difficult.

The following steps will help:

STEP 1 Provide clear and concise information about succession planning and its importance

STEP 2 Be prepared to answer all questions

STEP 3 Provide a prototype that shows functions and actions

STEP 4 Let each area of the organization see how it will affect them

STEP 5 Provide evidence of success for others

STEP 6 Describe support and resources that will be available

STEP 7 Describe opportunities for feedback and rewards

STEP 8 Other: _____

_____

_____

_____

_____

_____

3

Defining Responsibilities to the Program

"It is the direction and not the magnitude which is to be taken into consideration."

—Thomas Troward

DEFINING RESPONSIBILITIES AND FUNCTIONS

The challenge in this part of the plan is to review and allocate resources and personal responsibilities to the program. As in any strategic plan, priorities must be made explicit, policy and procedures defined and individuals and groups directed and motivated toward the action defined in the plan. Designing and assigning roles helps to implement the strategy.

Support from top executives is crucial, because senior executives can influence many people continuously and persuasively. Your structure of the strategic plan will frame role responsibilities, communications and working relationships, which specify how the work of the plan is divided and coordinated.

Plans succeed if all elements work together smoothly and without conflict, but in the real world, conflict is ever present. Your odds are greater for success if you have a clear understanding of what is expected to happen and when and if functions are outlined in such a manner that each individual understands what to do, when to do it, the resources allocated and how this role fits into the big picture.

THE START OF A SUCCESSION PLAN

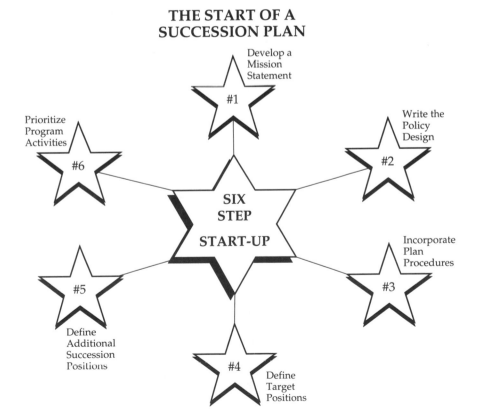

Develop a Mission Statement
#1

Write the Policy Design
#2

Prioritize Program Activities
#6

SIX STEP START-UP

Incorporate Plan Procedures
#3

Define Additional Succession Positions
#5

Define Target Positions
#4

DEFINE RESPONSIBILITIES

First, communicate to everyone what they are supposed to do. Nothing will get started until people know what is expected of them.

However, it isn't enough for succession planning participants to know what they will do; they must know why they are doing it, how it relates to the plan and the goals and objectives of the succession planning program. Just as every goal has a sense of purpose, each activity must offer a sense of purpose for those performing the responsibilities. Answers to the following questions will help clarify roles.

Questions to Ask

1. How do they view their roles for the successful establishment of a systematic succession planning program?

_____

_____

2. What roles should facilitators play in the program?

_____

_____

3. In addition to supporting the program, what else can management do to ensure the plan's success?

_____

_____

4. What activities would help the company move closer toward meeting its succession goals?

_____

_____

Succession planning standards should be consistent with company-wide standards. Encourage people to ask for clarification of their roles if they don't know what is expected of them.

#1: Develop the Mission

Every plan, every program, every strategy should begin with a clear sense of purpose—the mission. The mission statement for the succession planning program is not unlike a mission statement for an organization in that it addresses

- Why does this plan exist?

- What will the plan accomplish?

- How does it fit into the big picture?

- What is expected as a result of the plan?

- Who does the plan affect?

The statement you develop will be specific and designed to serve your organization.

Where to Start

Begin with a focus on discovery. Answer the questions on pages 42–43 to put you on track. Use the worksheet *again* and *again* to gather as much information as you need that will contribute to a sound mission acceptable by all.

DEFINE RESPONSIBILITIES (continued)

Answer and Discuss

1. Why are we developing a strategic succession plan? What is the driving force for this change?

_____

_____

2. Is it important that we do this? What might happen if we don't?

_____

_____

3. How should our company fill and replace valuable key positions?

_____

_____

4. What are our goals for having key positions backed by a successor?

_____

_____

5. How will we all benefit?

_____

_____

6. Is support available?

_____

_____

7. What type of training is available for high-performance individuals?

_____

_____

8. What type of development should be available?

_____

_____

9. What are the barriers to this change?

_____

_____

10. What can be done to overcome the barriers?

_____

_____

11. How do we track individual career goals and development?

_____

_____

12. What can be done to help prevent a high turnover of our exemplary performers?

_____

_____

13. Will the program plan be published to all employees?

_____

_____

14. Who will monitor the plan?

_____

_____

✳   ✳   ✳

You can have others contribute questions to the worksheet. This form of discovery is good when decision makers are scattered throughout the organization and it is difficult to bring them together. As with any information-gathering approach, distribute the results to all who participate.

DEFINE RESPONSIBILITIES (continued)

#2: Write the Policy

You have developed a good understanding for the reasons to implement a succession planning program. Now it is time to put it in writing, which can be done only when the mission is decided.

The policy can be defined as the broad statement of intent that communicates what is permitted or expected. Effective planning of successors cannot be achieved without clear and consistent policy guidelines. Use the following checklist for policy formulation.

Check off each that has been included.

☐ What implications of the succession plan need to be communicated?

☐ What areas of the plan need to be stressed?

☐ What assumptions need to be communicated?

☐ Is there a need to rule on possible situations that could arise?

☐ Are limits to be imposed?

☐ What is the company committed to doing regarding succession?

Keep policy statements concise. They should represent support of action to be followed. They should leave little room for doubt. Do not make them too long, cover too much ground, raise more questions than answers, leave no direction for procedures or sound too authoritative. Your policy should reflect consensus and be based on the company's capabilities and objectives toward the succession plan.

#3: Incorporate Plan Procedures

The plan's procedures direct how the policy will be followed. They represent guidelines necessary to carry out the plan's intent. Procedures offer written agreement on the action to be taken by the organization to insure commitment to succession planning. List and discuss procedures for your company's succession program. For example: "The organization will assure that performance assessments include future possibilities for individuals at all management levels."

Develop procedures that may work for your company.

1. _____

2. _____

3. _____

4. _____

5. _____

Now Formulate Your Procedure Statement:

> 66 _____
> _____
> _____
> _____
> _____
> _____
> _____ 99 .

46

DEFINE RESPONSIBILITIES (continued)

#4: Define Target Positions

For many years organizations focused only on management positions for their succession efforts. The CEO has almost always been a priority for most organizations. Succession planning may be carried out for many positions within your company, but a strategic program will have both initial positions identified and the percentage of effort for other areas, including development efforts. Use the list below to guide your decision on succession areas.

Area	Priority	Individual Area Developed
CEO		
President/top executives		
Vice presidents		
Assistant vice presidents		
Staff management		
Supervisors		
Sales		
Technicians		
Service		
Clerical		

#5: Define Additional Succession Positions

After you have chosen initial targets, define other groups to include in the succession planning effort. Often the groups are targeted because of a need to increase strength in that work area or to prioritize the succession groups. For example, it may be difficult to fill highly skilled technical positions because of requirements or certification that must be met. If one of these positions is lost and no successor has been trained, production losses could be enormous.

#6: Prioritize Program Activities

Activities that support both short- and long-term goals are needed. Activities are to be assigned a high, medium or low priority and target start and finish dates.

Suggested Activities

✓ Develop a guide for the start-up

✓ Distribute the plan

✓ Advise all involved of their roles

✓ Plan an introduction meeting for the program

✓ Provide information on possible succession planning problems and how to handle them

✓ Communicate program requirements

✓ Define all job requirements for positions involved in the target groups

✓ Review individual performance and potential

✓ Design and keep performance records

✓ Design and implement development plans

✓ Evaluate and assess the present and future

✓ Prepare for organizational changes with contingencies

DEFINE RESPONSIBILITIES (continued)

Can you think of additional activities or needs your organization should add to the list?

1. _____

2. _____

3. _____

Use the following chart to organize your activities.

Priority Chart

Activity	Priority	Long Term or Short		Comments
		Long	Short	

CASE STUDY:
Initial Start-Up

The Dryden Corp. used the "ask, formulate, and establish" approach to develop and start their succession planning program. First, the succession director developed an extensive questionnaire related to opinions and ideas for succession and development programs. The questions were distributed to all decision makers and top management. The results were summarized and formulated into the succession mission statement. The next set of questions clarified what the organization needed and wanted to do about succession and how policy would be applied. These results and statements were developed into policies and procedures that all agreed on. If needed, Dryden executives altered or changed these procedures as they proceeded. Once the executives were in agreement, they set up their initial targets for the program. This was helped by the succession director presenting a list of company positions. The executives then prioritized these positions in order of their importance to the operations of the company. They also gave their reasoning to the ratings. They chose three position groups to target initially: top executives, sales associates and managers, and then they worked with service managers. They voted on forms and methods by which to track the progress. Their options were provided by the succession committee they set up during the initial stages of development and commitment. They set up the action steps and their completion dates. This was just a beginning for the Dryden Corp. but they were on the right track. Over the years their success in their initial start-up proved to be the key to their long-term succession program success.

DEVELOP A STRATEGIC ACTION PLAN

Your list of activities and their priority is a good beginning, but only a start in the making of a succession plan. Your next step is your strategic action plan which describes the action to be taken for each activity and includes:

- Who takes the action
- When the action is performed
- How the action is performed
- Where to perform the action
- Why the action is needed
- What is the strategy

Not only is the activity listed, but the plan will show who is responsible for the outcome and where and when this is to happen. In developing the strategic action in this manner, you will leave little room for doubt about the details. Top decision makers and management involved in the program should all participate in developing the action plan. Consensus on the details is necessary for success.

Implementation Plan Worksheet

Priority Activity	Action Steps	Process Owner	Place	Dates

COMMUNICATING THE PROCESS

Effective communication is vital to the success of the succession plan. Some companies choose to keep the program's plan only in the hands of the decision makers, while many companies choose an "open" communication process. Open communications enhance employee involvement. With empowering programs and efforts toward self-directed teams, employees probably are better off knowing future possibilities. Other approaches include communicating the program's intent, design and activities without circulating information about who the successors will be. The communication design for the succession plan will depend on the company's overall communication history and preferences. The decision makers should all agree on the format.

Joining Forces

During the initial stages of succession planning, several meetings are required to lay the foundation. After the need is established by top decision makers, later meetings should be scheduled by the succession planning director, coordinator or leader to evaluate and report. This person must have the authority that accompanies the responsibility of organizing such activity.

Decision makers and executives should formulate a plan of action for the program. The committee should maintain the same goals for each meeting. The program director may hold the responsibility for the final development that committee members support. Sometimes consultants are hired to facilitate the program, keep it on track, and provide direction.

Off and Running

Once all committee members have approved your proposal, you should organize your introduction meeting. Before announcing a kick-off seminar, decide:

✓ Who is to attend

✓ How much participants will be told about their roles at this time

✓ What is the best timing to start the program formally

✓ Who will announce the commitment (CEO is the best option)

✓ How long the seminar will last

✓ When more details will be introduced

COMMUNICATION THROUGH TRAINING

Incorporate training into the planning process. The training effort should be designed around the program's priorities.

Participants at all levels will be involved in some form of training as it relates to succession planning. The initial training is geared toward those who will *play a role in the action plan.* Training must explain or offer:

- Clarification on the importance of succession planning

- How strategic succession planning works

- Coaching and counseling skills

- Performance appraisal skills

- Motivation through individual assessment

- Strategies for individual development

- The organization's role

- Procedures

- Approaches to individual talent recognition

- The evaluation process

- Alternatives to promoting from within

What other training issues would you include for your participants?

1. _____

2. _____

3. _____

4. _____

5. _____

SECTION

4

Identifying
Key Positions

"The barriers are not erected which can say to aspiring talents and industry, 'thus far and no farther.'"

—Ludwig Van Beethoven

IDENTIFYING KEY LEADERSHIP POSITIONS

Identifying key leadership positions in your organization may sound easy, but for many it is not. For many organizations, the organizational chart represents the leaders and their positions. A chart can be important, but it should not be used to identify talented employees or valued positions in a company. Other methods are more effective.

What Are Key Positions?

Key positions are not always obvious. Just because a "top-charted title" has been around for years doesn't mean that this position is crucial to the mission of the company. It would be nice to think that all positions are key to the success of the organization, but for the succession plan, key position is a position within the organization that provides significant importance in the strategic and operational decisions that affect organizational success.

These positions are not always at the top, but because critical operational decisions are often made in that traditional manner, many key positions are with top executives. Other key leadership positions are distributed throughout the organization—positions that, if left unfilled, would cause problems for the functions of the company, including production, sales, distribution, systems, purchasing or service. Three of the main reasons why positions must be identified separately in every company include:

1. Work distribution is different in every organization and even in like departments of different regions for the same organization.

2. Every company has its own set of standards and priorities.

3. Every company is different in market, size, and strengths.

IDENTIFYING KEY POSITION CRITERIA

Key positions can be evaluated and identified by several criteria.

▶ **CRITICAL TASK**

Any position that would stop critical action from taking place if it were left vacant. If this function did not happen, the organization would suffer.

▶ **SPECIALIZED LEADERSHIP**

Any position that requires a specialty or expertise.

▶ **ORGANIZATIONAL STRUCTURE**

Company history and structure can define some key positions. If a company has always had a vice president and it is known that the duties are required for the company's mission, the position itself can explain its importance.

▶ **FUTURE PROJECTS**

A highly competitive company often recruits for future needs before present duties are considered. High-tech companies often recognize future positions and consider the "function to be," not the duties for today.

▶ **GEOGRAPHICAL**

Geographical situations can lead to key position redundancy. It must be determined if the same jobs in different locations are needed, or if another alternative is available.

▶ **WORK LOAD**

Is a position key because it relieves others to make valuable decisions, or is the position part of the process by which decisions are made? If a position is only relief, then perhaps other practices should be considered before designating this a "key position."

A company can use many techniques to identify its key positions, but a format should be followed to maintain an objective and consistent approach. Answer the additional questions on page 57 as you establish your tracking system.

EXERCISE:
Questions to Think About

1. What are the requirements for each identified key position in our organization?

2. What personnel are in the key positions?

3. Is anyone available to replace a key position if it became vacant?

4. Do we know the retirement or career plans of individuals in key positions?

5. How are individuals evaluated in their leadership positions?

6. What are the job duties for each key position?

7. Where are the key positions located in the organization?

POSITION ANALYSIS

Job descriptions are not enough to decide what is required in these key positions. In reviewing each position outline position activities, individual responsibilities, team responsibility, necessary duties, required functions and complete task activity list.

In describing the job, you detail the work-related duties and activities. In describing the position, detail the activities and responsibilities of the individual doing the job.

Define the Dimensions

1. Review the organizational information of the job.
2. Review published information on similar jobs.
3. Interview incumbents to determine how they view the job compared to the original description given to them.
4. Interview executives to find out what has made others succeed or fail in the job.
5. Ask what critical incidents have been involved in the job.
6. Identify training issues related to the job.
7. Identify the requirements needed for the individual to do the job successfully.
8. Describe title, salary and level for the job function.
9. Determine what qualities and values the jobholder must have.

For each key position, start your thinking by listing the following:

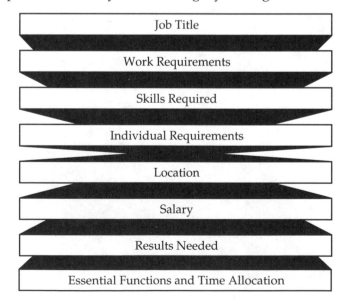

Job Title

Work Requirements

Skills Required

Individual Requirements

Location

Salary

Results Needed

Essential Functions and Time Allocation

As you develop key position descriptions, have them reviewed by all decision makers and the job incumbent. Use the following worksheet for each position.

Worksheet

Title _____ Salary Range _____

Location _____

Mission Statement _____

_____

Reporting _____

_____

Goals _____

_____

_____

Responsibilities _____

_____

_____

Activities _____

_____

_____

Position descriptions need to be revised and updated periodically to meet the changing activities of the organization, which not only helps the decisions for leadership continuity, but keeps employees informed to meet their requirements. Comply with any legal constraints when using these descriptions as a tool in recruiting and performance appraisals. A well-designed position description can provide many benefits to an organization, including identifying future training needs, work requirements and future determinations; assessing performance; and recruiting.

DETERMINING ESSENTIAL CHARACTER QUALITIES

Today's succession planning also calls for an assessment of the character qualities needed for the leadership positions. Each position should have its own requisite of the characteristics needed for that particular leadership role.

When looking for exceptional talent in successors, a company can benefit greatly by having character qualities outlined for the position. Many people are trained and qualified for specific jobs, but exemplary performance can often be identified by additional personal qualities. Distinguishing one potential successor from another can be left to subjective decision making if specific competencies are not included in the position requirements.

General Leadership and Management Qualities

- Good planner
- Organized
- Solid ethics
- Goal-oriented
- Communication skills
- Problem solver
- Team-oriented
- Decisive
- Creative
- Trustworthy
- Reliable
- Motivates
- Cares
- Responsible
- Innovative
- Negotiator
- Sincere

- Approachable
- Involved
- Growth-oriented
- Committed
- Detail-oriented
- Good facilitator
- Teacher
- Coach
- Empowering
- Tough
- Visual
- Confident
- Experienced
- Needs-oriented
- Focused
- Has integrity
- Competent

- Confronts problems
- Calm and collected
- Persuasive
- Risk taker
- Balanced life
- Solid values
- Dedicated
- Excellent attitude
- Rewards others
- Disciplinary
- High expectations
- Reasonable
- Open
- Positive
- Strong desire
- Takes initiative

Add to the list with additional management and leadership qualities that you believe a potential successor must have. Remember that not all qualities will be needed for all positions. Linking the necessary characteristics to the leadership position can be the key to exemplary performance.

Your List

- _____

- _____

- _____

The generic list should reflect your corporate culture and values. Applying the list of qualities to applicable job positions can be confusing if not done properly. Gathering decision makers and adding the needed characteristics to each position as the job is defined is the best approach. A consultant can facilitate the process in large organizations, and the assessment can be applied to jobs other than key positions to help maintain consistency in an organization. In succession planning programs, this systematic process can help a company establish guidelines in the continuous development and recognition of champions.

The Circle of Leadership

Leadership should be a continuous process for every company that commits to a succession plan. Leadership continuity is a process that requires six major steps. To ensure your commitment to leadership quality follow this "Circle of Leadership" process.

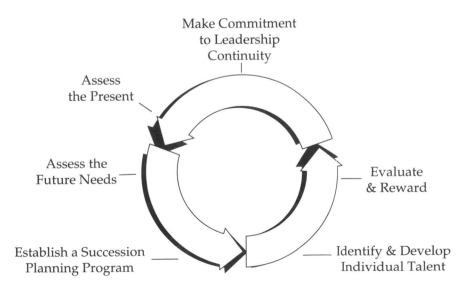

EVALUATING INDIVIDUAL PERFORMANCE

Dreaded by most employees, the performance appraisal process remains a constant in the corporate world. It has been attacked by experts, criticized by the creators themselves and still remains one of the most important sources for employee performance information. It is also a valuable tool for succession planning.

The Connection

Before you can link succession planning and performance evaluations, you must understand how appraisal differs from ordinary feedback and coaching.

- ► Advanced preparation goes into a performance appraisal

- ► Performance appraisal covers more ground and is more inclusive than coaching

- ► Performance appraisal usually takes place at a set time and place

- ► Performance appraisal follows an organized format

In succession planning, the purpose of review is not to fix blame, scare people into action, or hold people back. The appraisal should be used to demonstrate an individual's potential. The appraisal is geared toward future improvements based on present performance. This design offers freedom to look at what an individual should do to advance into a leadership role.

CASE STUDY AHEAD . . .

CASE STUDY:
New Evaluations Needed

The Myson Corp. knew that their present evaluation process was not going to hold up for the new succession planning program. They did not want management succession left to chance, favoritism or seniority. The organization set up a means to compare present job performance to future potential. The use of new feedback forms and structured interviews was chosen to validate present ability, and future potential was assessed by a performance appraisal form. This is usually conducted several months before the annual performance appraisal. The timing is such that it is not confused with past or present job performance. Employees and managers complete the forms and meet to discuss the future possibilities of both perceived and believed potential of the employee. This way, Myson's CEO believes that each employee learns of all the possibilities and of his or her strengths and weaknesses for possible advancement. No promises are made, and this works for the company and the employee.

Preparation Worksheet

Position and job-related responsibilities	Measurement of the activity
1.	
2	
3.	
4	
5.	
6.	

EVALUATING TEAM PERFORMANCE

Measuring and evaluating a team and team member's performance is also important to the succession planning process. This process helps an organization look at leadership qualities on a group performance basis and individual accomplishments using peer assessments. This works well for many organizations operating self-directed teams and team-based departments.

First, there should be a solid system for measuring and evaluating how the team is doing as a unit. Team measurements are based on team goals that fit into the divisions and organizational goals.

Second, every team should set individual performance standards for the team members as they relate to each project. Handled correctly, peer assessments are powerful forms of appraisal and can merge into the succession planning program. An organization must be well established in a team culture before using team or peer assessments as an evaluation or performance measurement. For the link to succession planning, the team-based individual performance reviews the following factors:

► **FLEXIBILITY:** Individual action to requests. Balance assignments and maintain priorities. Taking the extra step without complaining.

► **SUPPORTIVENESS:** Individual ability to solicit support and provide it where needed.

► **CREATIVITY:** Develops innovative solutions to problems and offers new and better ways to approach tasks.

► **INITIATIVE:** High energy and self-starter. Takes action without direction.

► **TRUSTWORTHY:** Reliable and friendly. Builds trust with others in and out of the work group.

► **ENTHUSIASTIC:** Presents an excellent attitude and is a spirited player that motivates others.

As you can see, the team player factors are high leadership qualities. This is one reason team assessment works well in succession selection.

The Peer Feedback Form on page 65 can be used by team members to help with assessment. The recorded comment section can then be designed on a measurement scale for final reviews, if desired.

Peer Feedback Form

Name of Team Member _____

Topic	Comment
1. Motivation	_____
2. Contributions	_____
3. Willingness to learn	_____
4. Cooperation	_____
5. Interpersonal skills	_____
6. Expertise	_____
7. Innovations	_____
8. Dependable	_____
9. Tactful	_____
10. Supportive	_____
11. Attitude	_____
12. Communication	_____
13. Contributions	_____
14. Understands	_____
15. Problem solving	_____
16. Productive	_____
17. Teaches	_____
18. Technical skills	_____
19. Quality	_____
20. Timeliness	_____

SECTION

5

Forecasting
Future Needs

"The secret of success in life is for a man to be ready for his opportunity when it comes."

—Benjamin Disraeli

PREDICTING FUTURE NEEDS

Organizations change constantly and predictions for the future are increasingly difficult to make. Staying on top of future needs can be a full-time job. For succession planning directors, the job is a difficult one. Not only are requirements a challenge to predict, but individual talent changes almost daily.

Succession Planning Forecasting

Organizational Exam

*Review the strategic planning process
the company uses*

Outside Factors

*Determine the factors outside of the organization that
can be expected to have an effect on hiring conditions*

Inside Factors

*Determine the factors within the control of the
organization that will affect personnel*

Estimate

*Estimate the effect these influences
will have on the company*

Much of the value and accuracy of the succession planning forecast depends on the ability of the executives to identify factors that will influence position needs, but everyone within the organization must be sensitive to outside factors that can affect the company.

PREDICTING FUTURE NEEDS (continued)

Uncertainty about the future has forced the strategic planning of many organizations to become more resilient to the environmental changes around them. As you review your company's plan, look at its assumptions in the following areas:

► Economy

Review relevant economic conditions, including general inflation, specific price trends or interest rates.

► Industry

Review industry trends. Look at the projected changes your company will have to make in regards to competitive position, new technologies, growth and status.

► Market

Review the projected market trends, including expected changes in demand for your product or service. A projection of customer needs and competitor's actions should be included if they apply.

► Outside Influences

Other factors that affect your company can influence the need for leadership, including governmental laws and regulations.

Use the worksheet on page 71 to examine external conditions that could affect your company in the next five years. Identify the trends for each area and predict their effect on your organization. Include function and position you think will be affected.

Environmental and External Conditions

Plan Assumptions for:

TREND	EFFECT
ECONOMY **1.** **2.** **3.** **4.**	
INDUSTRY **1.** **2.** **3.** **4.**	
MARKET **1.** **2.** **3.** **4.**	
OUTSIDE INFLUENCES **1.** **2.** **3.** **4.**	

POSITIONING THE JOBS

From the organizational forecasting plan, a company should understand the potential for principle position changes. New positions will emerge and old ones may change their responsibilities or be phased out. From the results you compiled in the previous environmental worksheet, you can now list the effects these trends will have on the work required in the company. You can take several approaches in conducting this analysis. You can interview top strategists in the company, bring together decision makers and key executives for group sessions or combine the two efforts.

Use the following worksheet to indicate the functions in the company that are most likely to be affected by the future trends and how that work will change. Use one worksheet for each position you identify for the future. Compare future job requirements with your past and present descriptions, and include performance standards.

Worksheet

Principle Position _____

Position Objective _____

Position Requirements _____

_____

Expected Results _____

_____

Risk in Change _____

_____

Position Activities _____

_____

Performance Standards _____

_____

SELECTING YOUR DREAM TEAM

Your next step is to identify future leaders and their potential at every level of the organization. Begin with an old-fashioned organizational chart. Remember that this is a *future chart*. Try variations of the structure as you work your way through this assessment.

Future Charting Sample

ASSESSING INDIVIDUAL POTENTIAL

Assessing employee potential and identifying leadership ability is not always easy. Some employees simply stand out. They have the highest potential for future leadership because of their exceptional performance. Other employees contribute in other ways. To assess potential, workers can be categorized in four ways.

► **Stars**—These exceptional performers have the greatest potential for advancement.

► **Supporting Roles**—These individuals can be developed for starring roles. Their performance needs work, but the possibilities are there.

► **Production Crew**—These individuals are exceptional in what they do, but show little interest or potential for other activities. They should remain motivated and productive as long as their skills are kept current in the work they do well.

► **Extras**—If extras are present in your company, make every effort to help them improve; if they don't, termination may be the only solution. These individuals do not have advancement possibilities and their present performance does not enhance the company's position.

CASE STUDY: High Potential—Wrong Position

Mary Elder had been recognized as an exemplary employee long before she was noted as a high potential employee. With this recognition came the opportunity for a new position. Mary was slated as the next v.p. of operations. This planned promotion initiated a three-year individual development plan that was designed to have her ready to assume the responsibilities of v.p. of operations once the current v.p. retired. Problems began in the early part of the first year of development, and the executives began to question her readiness. Their vital mistake: The problems had nothing to do with Mary's ability, but more to do with her desire. They had assumed that Mary would want this advancement, but she had no interest. She was perfectly happy as district manager and had reached satisfaction in her career. High potentials must want the new job before they are trained or developed for a specific leadership position.

EVALUATING INDIVIDUALS FOR FUTURE OPPORTUNITIES

Planning for the future cannot be done without planning criteria. Formulating a means to assess individual future potential is necessary. Exceptional performance in the present is a start for the assessment, but it does not always reflect future potential. An organization must determine what practices are to be assessed for future advancement opportunities and how well one must perform before additional development can take place.

The Feedback Process

Do your employees want to be leaders? You better ask them. One approach is the interview/survey instrument. The advantage to developing your own over using a standard form is that you can apply practices specific to your organization. A commercial questionnaire may be too generic, but can be used as a guide and tailored to your needs. Gathering information about the individual can be done by interviews and written survey. You may wish to formulate your questions based on your company's leadership practices.

SECTION

6

Assessing Your Organization's Climate

“There is no stimulus like that which comes from the consciousness of knowing that others believe in us.”

—Orson Swett Morden

CREATING A CLIMATE FOR LEADERS

Creating a climate in which leaders can develop, thrive and grow is a vital part of succession planning. Corporate culture affects not only individual performance, but also the performance and growth of the organization as a whole.

Climate describes the work environment and the collective human interaction of the employees. If you think about your company, you can probably describe its climate and the factors that contribute to that climate. What is the company philosophy, and do you fit in?

Corporate culture is often influenced by the structure of the organization, the actions of its management and the attitude of its employees. Positive attitude in a work environment can encourage high potential employees to accomplish great things. Company leadership develops a positive growth climate for their successors. A continued sense of purpose and accomplishment creates performance energy, which can be a great change motivator. Individuals adapt to the changes as they experience positive results.

Dimensions of Climate

Let's examine the six most valuable dimensions of organizational climate and divide them into two main categories:

ACTION DIMENSIONS and *FUNCTIONAL DIMENSIONS*

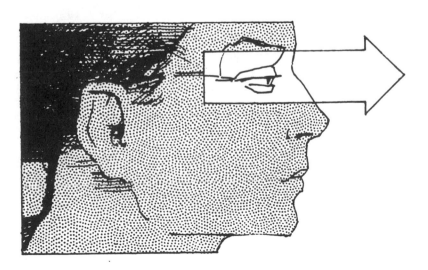

CREATING A CLIMATE FOR LEADERS (continued)

Action Dimensions

The three action dimensions are understanding, standards and empowerment.

► **UNDERSTANDING**

The clarity of the organization's policies and goals for employees and the extent to which they understand the job requirements and total responsibility.

► **STANDARDS**

The emphasis placed on exceptional performance and the commitment to every project.

► **EMPOWERMENT**

Individual commitment to goal achievement and self-direction for high standards.

Functional Dimensions

The three functional dimensions are recognition, support and accountability.

► **RECOGNITION**

How people feel about receiving credit for excellent performance. Rewards are clear and timely.

► **SUPPORT**

Teamwork: strength, respect and support given to each other.

► **ACCOUNTABILITY**

Whether people feel responsible for contributions they make toward the organization's goals. The individual's judgment is trusted by others and initiative is encouraged.

Climate Control Assessment

These statements can have a direct relationship to the leadership climate in an organization. You decide to what extent your company participates in creating a climate for potential leaders.

	Agree	Disagree
1. New ideas are encouraged.	☐	☐
2. Quality work is required and supported.	☐	☐
3. Team spirit is at every level.	☐	☐
4. New information is shared with all employees.	☐	☐
5. Rewards are given for high performance.	☐	☐
6. People "work the problem," not go around it.	☐	☐
7. Leaders take responsibility for making a decision.	☐	☐
8. Change is communicated in a positive manner.	☐	☐
9. Performance measurement is fair and objective.	☐	☐
10. Employees receive feedback and help when needed.	☐	☐
11. Departments work well together.	☐	☐
12. People are motivated and committed to excellence.	☐	☐
13. Communication is frank and honest.	☐	☐
14. People feel secure in speaking up.	☐	☐
15. Procedures are clear.	☐	☐
16. Each employee affects quality and productivity.	☐	☐
17. Relationships are good within the departments.	☐	☐
18. Goals are realistic and attainable.	☐	☐
19. Employee development is supported.	☐	☐
20. There is positive influence in the company.	☐	☐

If you disagree with most of these statements, your organization's climate may need adjustment before leadership can be fostered.

PRESENTING A VISION OF LEADERSHIP

A good, solid climate and culture take time to build and must adapt to changing conditions. All company leaders should display commitment to the organization's common purpose, develop and reward competence in key areas and remain consistent in their actions. The combination of strategy and culture allows leaders to commit themselves to the long term. The opportunity for advancement presents employees with a vision of the future. In succession planning, a positive vision is required before development can create a reality for the talented individuals in the organization. No two companies are identical, and no two will tackle creating a leadership climate in just the same way.

Maximizing Management

Exceptional individuals are valuable assets for companies who need to maximize their employees' efforts at a time when they might be consolidating sites and laying off workers. Companies can accelerate the development of these valuable individuals. An accelerated program is a systematically planned effort designed for employees who have been chosen for potential advancement. The programs are long-term commitments by both the employee and the company.

Many accelerated development programs cannot be called by that name. First, the company usually does not make a promise of advancement once the program is completed. Second, individuals not included in the "accelerated program" may feel unempowered and left out of any advancement, which is not the case.

Accelerated programs may be called management or executive development, leadership skills, assistant management or diversification executive program, supervisory skills training or empowerment program but, no matter what a company calls it, the program is designed to accelerate highly talented individuals by increasing their expertise to meet the company's growing needs.

A company may design the program internally or use an outside source. Some programs consist of sending the individuals for advanced degrees, a series of planned seminars, planned mentoring and other development techniques. Many companies combine programs with time frames that fit the future succession assignment. For any accelerated program to be a success, it must engage the personal attention of the individual and full involvement of the company.

Development Guidelines

The guidelines are simple, but complications occur if they are not followed.

1. Ensure personal commitment and support from all senior level personnel.

2. Have the program meet the strategic needs of the organization.

3. Structure the program to focus on the desired result for the individuals.

4. Use a variety of educational techniques and involve the talented individual in the selection process.

5. Remain flexible for unexpected changes.

All individuals selected for accelerated programs should perform useful, needed work while in development. Individual coaching and nurturing is part of the process of learning while performing. Job rotation can build the additional skills necessary.

NURTURING TALENT

Many companies fail to tap their employees' potential because often they reward them only with pay. To get the most from workers, a company must nurture a relationship between employer and leader that motivates, allows for growth, encourages and develops an exceptional talent into an exceptional leader. In fact, the company must spend more than money. But to nurture anyone, you must C-A-R-E.

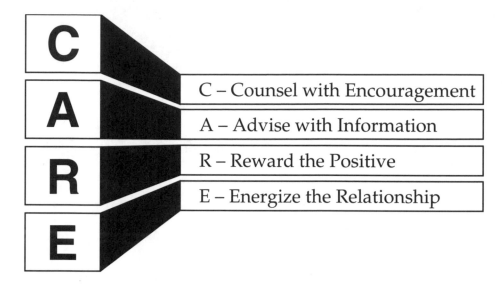

C – Counsel with Encouragement

A – Advise with Information

R – Reward the Positive

E – Energize the Relationship

COUNSEL WITH ENCOURAGEMENT

Encouragement is much more than a pat on the back. It motivates and generates growth toward an expectation and helps one reach full potential.

ADVISE WITH INFORMATION

A good mentor never takes over for another employee when things get difficult, but advises and allows the other to make an intelligent decision with the needed information.

REWARD THE POSITIVE

To maintain a level of exceptional performance, accomplishments that exceed expectations must be rewarded.

ENERGIZE THE RELATIONSHIP

Staying on top of things can destroy the momentum of any leader. In a cooperative workplace, leaders and high potential workers can be energized with resources and a support system.

PROVIDING THE RIGHT TOOLS

If you want people to grow with the company, you need to provide the proper resources. Tools include more than state-of-the-art equipment. Providing leaders with information, ideas, mentoring, coaching, and rewards is all part of the succession process. Companies must also equip talented employees with support and communication. Communication can assist in the transfer of organization goals, practices and values. What tools do the future leaders of your company need?

Succession Planning Tools For Future Leaders

TOOLS	and their	USE
1.		
2.		
3.		
4.		
5.		
6.		
7.		
8.		
9.		
10.		

SUPPORTING LONG-TERM COACHING

Having the right players in your organization is vital, but having excellent coaching makes champions within your dream team. In leadership continuity, coaching is the interaction that directs any game plan. A good coach helps the players focus on the goal and teaches the fundamentals for success.

A good coach should:

- Communicate expectations
- Listen for adjustments
- Allow opportunity to develop
- Provide choices
- Instruct for improvement
- Reward results

A good coach will have to:

- Resolve political situations

- Get people to be problem solvers

- Work with other executives

- Negotiate in the company and outside

- Work with people who do not work for you

- See other points of view

- Handle conflict

- Motivate self and others

- Give credit to others

- Solve performance problems

- Communicate with your boss

A good coach* must have basic values: sensitivity, honesty, caring for coworkers. A good coach must be willing to share knowledge and be part of a team. A coach must be confident and strong and use power positively, because he or she must be able to build strong ideas that others accept, learn continuously, think consistently in the long term, set agendas, make plans and follow through on them through thick and thin. A good coach must do this while balancing a personal life, accepting limitations, taking steps toward his or her own goals, and fostering quality.

CASE STUDY: Coaching and Enabling

Paul Creasor, CEO of Spartan Technologies, knows that a good leader and coach has to let go. After training and providing frontline experience for every manager, he gives each full responsibility for his or her area of expertise. They are empowered to make decisions and their mistakes are viewed as learning experiences. Each manager is given the responsibility to develop teams, delegate authority and coach people toward discovering the answers for themselves. Creasor has shown the managers values, ethical and quality standards and guiding principles to follow. He says that the rest is up to them.

*For an excellent book on this topic, read *Coaching for Development* by Marianne Minor, Crisp Publications.

LEARNING TO FLY

Coaching is not just teaching; employees must eventually be given the opportunity to move on their own and make their own decisions. Without the opportunity to fly alone, people cannot lead; they will not make a difference. Although coaching begins with encouragement, support and rewards, the most effective means of self-confidence is through experience. Remember, however, that assigning tasks without delegating responsibility will not foster leadership skills.

Continuous Improvement

Employees must work every day on improving the company and themselves. It is a continuous journey, and the individuals focus on the big picture, as does the succession plan.

The need for improvement does not mean overloading talented workers because you believe they can do the additional work. Many managers make this mistake after corporate restructuring. To have individuals and the organization continuously improve, leaders will want to do all they can to avoid the loss of key talent from the company.

To Help Avoid Loss

► Plan carefully and monitor workload redistribution efforts

► Ask talented employees about their progress

► Address complaints and feelings of pressure

► Make sure there is time for development

► Address turnover problems

► Be sure the succession plan is followed

IMPROVING WITH TEAMS

Many companies have a well-established team environment. Although we speak of talented employees as individuals performing as future leaders, it is the combined skills of leaders that make an organization a success.

The team effort can produce an additional talent pool for a company. Effective leaders of high-performing teams know how to support teams by coaching, counseling, training, removing barriers and listening. The most talented members of a team can improve motivation, satisfaction and productivity of others and help develop a multitalented employee base. From this base, an organization can pool employees from different groups to solve problems and work on special projects. The increase of cross-trained talent can keep a company from simply replacing a vacant position; they can make a succession decision based on skill, performance and potential. Use the worksheet to plan your team succession efforts.

Worksheet

Team Members and Area of Responsibility	Cross-Training Completed
1.	
2	
3.	
4.	
5.	
6.	
7.	

SECTION

7

Promoting Employees: The Search From Within

"*There is always room at the top.***"**

—David Webster

FINDING THE STRENGTH FROM WITHIN

The obvious objective of succession planning is to establish a systematic means for replacing key personnel with strong incumbents. It is not enough to identify the positions, people and work responsibilities; A company needs to include both *personal development planning* and *planned program development*.

Still, sometimes internal promotion is not the answer to succession. Events or policies can weaken an organization's ability to promote from within. People quit, weakening a company's promotion efforts. Planned cutbacks, including layoffs, joint ventures, and reengineering can create serious problems for leadership in key positions. Executive resignations can create a management crisis if a company does not prepare for such events with succession planning. However, you can test your company's ability to handle this type of turnover stress.

ANALYZE → Reviewing the turnover records for each area for several years will help you understand how succession was accomplished, the problems the loss created and how fast the problems were resolved. If a successor was not obvious for the vacancy and time-consuming efforts were made to find a replacement, this is certainly a sign of weakness in key position replacement efforts that must be corrected.

INQUIRE → Ask the leaders in your organization how they would replace a key position in their area if it were to become vacant suddenly. Ask how they would fill the position if they knew it would become vacant within the year. Any gaps in their ability or preparedness to fill the position can be determined as a weakness for the company.

INVESTIGATE → Investigate any formal or informal policy for promoting and recruiting within the organization. If senior management does not follow or know the policy, you have a succession problem.

POSITION CHARTING → Position charting is a diagram of all possible openings for each key position. Any blanks on the chart indicate a problem.

TRACKING POTENTIAL SUCCESSORS

Using forms helps to maintain a consistent approach to the "strength from within" test. Executives must evaluate people and positions before individual development programs can be prepared. This evaluation exceeds performance appraisals and subjective recommendations. A professional development plan for a potential successor is an objective, collective analysis of the individual's strengths and weaknesses. Meeting internal promotion needs depends on how well the company prepares these individuals for advancement.

Position Charting Sample

KEY POSITION	ORDER OF SUCCESSORS
MARKETING DIRECTOR	#1. Mary Smith #2. Tom Allen #3. Jim Green
CHIEF FINANCIAL OFFICER	#1. _____ #2. _____ #3. _____
CHIEF LEGAL ADVISOR	#1. _____ #2. _____ #3. _____

ORDER: #1. Ready to assume position now.

#2. Ready in one to three years.

#3. Ready in three to five years.

Sample Position Planning Form
(Use for each position)

Name _____

Title _____

Performance Rating _____

Potential Rating _____

Current Status _____

Desired Status _____

REFINING YOUR INTERNAL PROMOTION POLICY

In systematic succession plans there is always, or at least there *should* always, be a written internal promotion policy. Internal promotion policy offers both a long-term protection plan and money-saving features for the prepared company. Although it does not cover a company for all unexpected personnel loss, it can provide a course of action for replacement of valuable individuals in the event of loss. With this policy in place, the organization shows key people that they are valued and have long-term opportunities.

Internal recruiting policy should meet the legal and strategic needs of the company. These guidelines suggest the outline for an internal promotion policy.

► The policy should state that all efforts will be made to fill key positions from within the company before outside approaches are considered.

► Explain internal promotion and key positions.

► Explain the strategic benefit to the company for internal promotion policy.

► Define all conditions before an external candidate will be considered for a key position.

► Explain the process that will be used to support the promotion-from-within policy.

► Explain the conditions under which the policy can be changed and alternative methods can be used.

To ensure that your policy complies legally and with all departments, the decision makers in the company should review it. They should commit to the policy, and communication should be open and understood. The policy should be included as a central piece of the succession program and as a part of the overall company plan.

Provisions

An internal promotion plan must contain the following provisions.

1. The succession candidate must be prepared to assume all duties and responsibilities for the key position. Readiness is determined by the decision makers after the individual has become proficient and demonstrated excellence in almost all the requirements of the position and completed an intense professional development plan.

2. When the position is vacated, the successor must be ready and willing to accept the responsibilities of that key position.

Proposed internal promotions that do not meet these provisions are inappropriate, and alternatives should be considered. Perhaps the proposed successor has not met the requirements, left the company unexpectedly or chooses not to make the job change. In that case, management should look outside the company to make the hire. However, the policy conditions must support the entire succession plan and not compromise the long-term course of action.

PROFESSIONAL DEVELOPMENT PLAN GUIDELINES AHEAD

PREPARING PROFESSIONAL DEVELOPMENT PLANS

Professional development is taken after an individual has been assessed in his or her job and potential for advancement has been identified. The professional development plan will bridge the gap between present ability and future requirements for key job positions. Management and employee commit to a complete learning agreement. The focus is not on one job or title, but on activities, functions, responsibilities, tasks and other related performance objectives.

The following guidelines can be used to prepare individual professional development plans.

Guidelines for Professional Development Plans

STEP 1   Know and identify the key positions for which you will develop the individual.

STEP 2   Identify the work requirements the individual must acquire.

STEP 3   Specify the activities for the development and learning objectives.

STEP 4   Set a time frame for completing each activity and total development program.

STEP 5   Specify how the activities will be conducted and how the learning objectives will be met. List the resources needed and how they will be obtained.

STEP 6   Establish evaluation methods to measure accomplishment and development.

STEP 7   Define how and who will assess the performance.

STEP 8 Have the professional development plan reviewed by experts who are qualified to determine the performance objectives.

STEP 9 Execute the plan and follow through with regular reviews and monitoring.

STEP 10 Evaluate the result and document the progress or deficiency. Discuss with the future successor.

Preparing for Professional Development

The following form can be used as a guide for preparing an individual for his/her development. The form should be filled out by those responsible for the advancement and discussed with the individual. Changes should be made as needed.

Successor's Name _____

Position _____

Time In Position _____

Key Position To Prepare For _____

Other Position Considerations _____

Individual's Career Goals _____

Development Objectives _____

Methods of Development _____

PREPARING PROFESSIONAL DEVELOPMENT PLANS (continued)

Sample Learning Objectives

1. _____ Date to Complete: _____

Measurement Method: _____

2. _____ Date to Complete: _____

Measurement Method: _____

Development Goal

The development process for most corporations involved in succession programs is to have their leaders eventually reach a level that allows them to handle or have the knowledge enabling them to manage all facets of the business. These are the individuals who make an impact far beyond their own individual capabilities. The growth pattern may look something like this:

DEVELOPMENT GROWTH PATTERN

6 _____ Can handle anything

5 _____ Can mentor others

4 _____ Growth to a higher level job

3 _____ Can do their job and more

2 _____ Can do their job well

1 _____ Basic abilities

INTERNAL PROFESSIONAL DEVELOPMENT

The organization's internal professional development plan consists of the activities offered inside the company that assist individuals toward their advancement.

CASE STUDY:
Planned Program Development

The Trace Oil Co. had suffered several waves of cutbacks and for several years had offered early retirement to eligible employees. Top executives knew that the company had become weak in all levels of management. They needed to take long-term corrective action, but, at first, they were unsure of how to go about this. One executive proposed a management training program and, after researching the parameters of the "leadership shortage" facing the company, proposed a management development program.

The company decision makers then surveyed management about their supervisory talent needs; based on these needs, the company recruited entry-level talent from inside and outside of the company. These individuals participated in a program designed to expose them to all facets of the company. They went to training classes on management topics for at least one afternoon each week. Present management also took the training and provided hands-on exercises for all.

After completing these structured programs, the participants rotated management activities. They were evaluated at every stage of their training. If improvement was not demonstrated, participants were removed from the program. After three years the program was a resounding success and the company's management team became stronger.

INTERNAL PROFESSIONAL DEVELOPMENT (continued)

Professional In-House Development Methods

- Public seminars

- On-site continuing education

- Mentoring

- In-house seminars

- Monitored self-study programs

- Intergroup development

- Advanced degree programs

- Job rotation

- On-the-job training

- Customized individual coaching

- Video and tapes

- Team process training

Internal methods can be very successful for professional development. Many of the learning objectives can be measured and learning controlled. Next we will focus on alternatives to internal methods.

SECTION

8

Choosing A Succession Planning Design

When defeat comes, accept it as a signal that your plans are not sound, rebuild those plans and set sail once more toward your coveted goal.

—Napoleon Hill

SELECTING SUCCESSION PLANNING DESIGNS

Each succession planning design has advantages and disadvantages, and each organization must decide which of these traditional and nontraditional approaches will satisfy their succession planning requirement, remembering that many approaches may be appropriate.

TRADITIONAL DESIGN

▶ New Hire Entry

▶ Promotion

▶ Transfers

▶ Demotion

▶ Employee Termination

▶ Positioned Career Development

NONTRADITIONAL DESIGN

▶ Reallocation

▶ Job Sharing

▶ Position Redesign

▶ Part-time Employees

▶ Contracting Out the Work

▶ Short-term Outsiders

▶ Talent Pools

▶ Diversified Assistant

▶ Recruiting

SELECTING SUCCESSION PLANNING DESIGNS (continued)

Traditional

▶ **NEW HIRE ENTRY.** One way to fill key positions is to hire off the street. This person may be a risk and create conflict, but also can bring fresh, new ideas to an organization.

▶ **TRANSFERS.** Moving an employee from one position to another nonrelated position can be a good way to fill a key position.

▶ **EMPLOYEE TERMINATION.** Not an attractive option, but it can be useful in eliminating unproductive workers.

▶ **PROMOTION.** A very traditional means of filling positions. Promoting from within is popular and effective if careful selections are made.

▶ **DEMOTION.** No one wants to go backward in their career, but it can be a way to preserve jobs and keep talented leadership.

▶ **POSITIONED CAREER DEVELOPMENT.** When opportunities are limited in an organization, individuals can be developed for the future while they perform their current job functions.

Nontraditional

▶ **REALLOCATION.** When a position is left vacant, the work is distributed to others and they can take on the responsibilities of that job. Be careful not to overload talented workers.

▶ **POSITION REDESIGN.** Not all vacant positions need to be replaced. In many reorganizing efforts, some positions become unnecessary.

▶ **CONTRACTING OUT THE WORK.** Bringing in expertise for projects is popular and sometimes employment is offered.

► **TALENT POOLS.** Developing talented individuals for several positions provides many options when a position requires filling.

► **RECRUITING.** The search for new talent can be made long before a position needs to be filled. Outsiders can be identified early for this and offered the job.

► **JOB SHARING.** Having two people perform one job works for some companies.

► **PART-TIME EMPLOYEES.** Often a position does not require a full-time employee.

► **SHORT-TERM OUTSIDERS.** Temps can fill in with great success and can be offered employment.

► **DIVERSIFIED ASSISTANT.** Having a "back-up"—an assistant who knows one job and learns others—works for some companies.

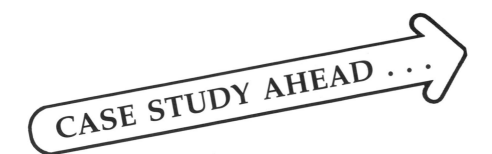

CASE STUDY AHEAD . . . .

CASE STUDY: A Nontraditional Approach

Leeland Space Corp. has had a senior executive and an assistant executive in their top positions for years. Leeland uses the assistant slot to move executives from one area of business to another to have them gain experience in all aspects of the company. It may seem like overstaffing to some, but it allows for personal development while preserving management continuity. Leeland has not had a disruption in operational procedures in many years, and the company contends that having an assistant slated for all executive positions provides leadership succession in all areas of the organization. The CEO states that all executives are trained for all jobs, and job rotation is part of the program. This leaves room for needed changes and unplanned losses on the team.

List some of the approaches you think would work well for your organization. Include any that you can think of that are not mentioned here.

Company Succession Options

1. _____

_____

2. _____

_____

3. _____

_____

4. _____

_____

5. _____

_____

CONSIDERATIONS TO REPLACING KEY POSITIONS

1. Is the position still needed?

A replacement is not always necessary just because a position has been on the organizational chart for years. Perhaps things have changed so much that the position and its responsibilities are no longer valuable to the company. If the decision makers find that the position no longer fits into the overall goals and objectives for the company, then it should be eliminated and no replacement needs to be found.

2. Is there another way?

Many companies have restructured their organizations, and positions have been eliminated because companies found new means to achieve their ends. To determine if jobs can be eliminated:

- Identify the process to improve

- Select a qualified team to work on the methods

- Identify the workflow and all areas affected

- List the factors of concern

- Develop a more efficient method

- Develop a means of evaluating the desired results

- Advise of needed changes

- Review and evaluate changes

With this process may also come new requirements and skills for the new work process.

CONSIDERATIONS TO REPLACING KEY POSITIONS (continued)

3. Is reallocating an option?

If the work duties can be redistributed to others in the department or to a team, then the position may not need a replacement. You must be able to obtain the same or better results if the choice is made, and all duties distributed must maintain the same importance as when the individual was responsible for them. Be careful not to overload the team.

4. Can other departments do the job?

If the work of a key position can be reassigned to another department or another function without compromising performance, then the position may not need to be filled.

5. Can the work be done by a contractor?

Contracting is not a new practice for companies and will always be a popular option if the work to be done does not require the control of someone inside of the company. Contractors are often used because of their overall expertise or skill in a defined area. If the duties are specific to your organization and you require internal specifications, then an inside permanent successor may be the better choice.

6. Is the work flexible but necessary?

Some job duties do not require a full-time person. Using part-time, temporary or even interns may fill the need and still maintain the job as it is required. Sometimes job rotation works well for this type of position.

EXERCISE: *Chart Your Options*

List any vacant positions in your organization that could use any of these approaches. Explain the alternatives for the duties, if applicable.

POSITION	ALTERNATIVE APPROACH	WORK REALLOCATION

Examine other key positions and assess if alternatives can be used to traditional replacement practices. In an alternate approach can be used, explain how and why.

1. Key Position _____

Traditional Approach or Alternative _____

Explain _____

2. Key Position _____

Traditional Approach or Alternative _____

Explain _____

3. Key Position _____

Traditional Approach or Alternative _____

Explain _____

CONSIDERATIONS TO REPLACING KEY POSITIONS (continued)

EXERCISE: Finding Alternatives

Start with five to ten *currently filled* positions and think above future needs and possibilities for each position. Check each listed alternative that might apply. Some positions may have several options.*

Position:

☐ **REALLOCATION:** When this position is left vacant, the work can be distributed to others and they will take on the responsibilities of that job.

☐ **POSITION REDESIGN:** Not all positions need a replacement; some positions are deemed unnecessary as a result of reengineering efforts.

☐ **CONTRACTING OUT THE WORK:** Bringing in outside expertise can lead to job offers for that person.

☐ **TALENT POOLS:** Developing talented individuals for several positions provides many options.

☐ **RECRUITING:** Searching for new talent can be done before this position is left vacant; hiring from another company or using "headhunters" is an option.

☐ **JOB SHARING:** We can use two people to perform one job.

☐ **PART-TIME EMPLOYEES:** Some duties can be performed on a part-time basis by part-time employees.

☐ **SHORT-TERM OUTSIDERS:** Trained temps can fill in when needed and be offered employment.

☐ **DIVERSIFIED ASSISTANT:** Assistants can know the job well and fill in when needed.

---

*This page be reproduced without further permission from the publisher.

EXERCISING FREEDOM TO CHOOSE SUCCESSORS

Companies must exercise their freedom to choose leaders on the basis of what is best for the organization. Even the greatest advocates of succession planning can have a difficult time adhering to their structure when changes force many high-level people to leave.

The best succession plans include the option of external hiring. This option must be adopted when loss has left no suitable successor to fill a critical position, although candidates may have been identified and developed. To recruit effectively from the outside, companies must:

- ► Understand the performance needed for the key position

- ► Define the job and its responsibilities

- ► Communicate the need and reasons for the outside search

- ► Specify the qualifications or requirements needed for the position

- ► Have a time frame for filling the position

- ► Have a list of possible candidates

- ► Have a list of sources to use

Knowing talented people on the outside is helpful when you are building and maintaining a high level of leadership possibilities. Your sources can be recruiters, competitive organizations, other companies, consultants and even former employees.

Keeping your options open is an important part of the succession plan. Remember that the future of your company depends upon your planning strategies.

TRACKING OPTIONS

The thought of creating more forms and paperwork is appalling for managers who already have far too much to do. Today, many software options can help organizations maintain performance records, succession planning and other policies. Many programs can merge management functions with employee records or files. Some of the features to look for:

- ► Helps develop at least a five-year plan

- ► Tracks succession planning

- ► Records training and development on an individual and group basis

- ► Tracks career planning

- ► Scans documents

- ► Permits data exchange

- ► Holds and helps develop job descriptions

- ► Generates status and planning reports

- ► Offers comparison activities

A study of each vendor will help you decide which program will work best for your organization. Always purchase a program that can expand to meet future requirements.

9

Analyzing Your Results

"The facts, if they are there,
speak for themselves."

—David Seabury

PROVIDING PROOF POSITIVE

Suppose someone in the organization challenges the need, worth or value of succession planning? What should you have to prove about it and how do you provide the proof? The main items to prove are:

- That the succession plan works

- That the results are worth the costs

- That the succession plan meets the organization's succession objectives

Proof is provided by:

- Evaluation

- Assessment

- Results

Evaluations

Just as with individual performance, you must evaluate all the dimensions of the succession planning program. To do this you must:

- ▶ Identify all areas to be evaluated

- ▶ Establish your benchmark for each dimension

- ▶ Review your data collection method and collect data

- ▶ Determine gaps in the program

- ▶ Compare all desired results with present findings

- ▶ Communicate findings

- ▶ Establish changes if needed

- ▶ Develop new action steps if needed

- ▶ Implement new actions and monitor progress

- ▶ Communicate progress

PROVIDING PROOF POSITIVE (continued)

The outcome of this continuous process should reflect that the succession plan contributes to the organization's strategic plan and vice versa. Too often the succession plan is evaluated only on how a vacancy was filled and how many were filled. This is not what succession planning is all about, and other factors must be considered to have accurate results.

A skilled evaluator should be appointed to direct the evaluation process, and additionally, an evaluation committee should work on certain components of the program. The succession planning director should take part in all areas of the evaluation process.

Asking the Right Questions

You must ask the right questions to evaluate your succession planning program. Depending on the depth and complexity of your program, your questions might include:

1. How well is each component of the program working?

2. Are the decision makers satisfied with the way the plan is working?

3. Are targeted leaders satisfied with the program?

4. Does the program support individual career plans as expected?

5. How well is the development and training working?

6. Does the program contribute to the competitive objective of the organization?

7. What organizational success has occurred as a result of the succession plan?

8. What organizational failures can be attributed to the plan?

9. Have key positions been filled in a more timely manner because of the plan?

10. Have more positions been filled because of the program?

11. Are the successors more effective in their new job roles because of the program?

12. What approaches to filling key positions have worked best as a result of the plan?

13. What savings can be documented from using the program's format rather than past means for filling key positions?

14. What complaints have been made about the program?

15. Has the program made a difference in unplanned turnover?

16. Has the program been useful in any planned losses of personnel?

17. What development strategies have worked best to prepare future leaders for their new roles?

18. Has there been any noticeable change in attitude since the program was implemented?

19. Has the program been difficult to monitor?

20. How well are the program directors performing their jobs?

Some of these questions require subjective analysis, which can be a difficult way to obtain a true value of the program. Still, subjective points of view are necessary and must be part of the evaluation process, because opinions do count.

PROVIDING PROOF POSITIVE (continued)

CASE STUDY:
Observation and Program Evaluations

Omni Systems, Inc. does not want to wait for the end of the year to know what is right or wrong with their succession planning program. Management believes that planned leadership is the key to success, so they meet with their succession management team once every quarter. They monitor every component of their program and each decision maker reviews all activities related to his or her part of the program. Brainstorming sessions are used to make revisions and add or delete from the program. The program's progress is always compared with the intended results. Reports are made and distributed throughout the company. The managers at Omni then review the action for the next six months, and any changes they make to the program are voted on. Every consideration is given to the changes that the company may be experiencing as a whole.

DISCOVERING CAUSE AND EFFECT

If you discover problems in the succession planning program, you must fix them. Find the major components under which the problem falls and list the effect and all possible causes that might have created the problem.

Cause and Effect Analysis Form

PROBLEM	CAUSE	EFFECT	SOLUTION

Observation

Observation is part of the evaluation process for any succession program. Leaders, decision makers, the succession director and evaluation committee members should all be aware that continuous observation of the program is required to make changes when needed. Both problems and successes should be noted. If there is an identifiable problem, focus on solving the problem, not the symptoms. Once problems are identified, the committee should brainstorm possible solutions or make design changes with a defined plan to implement the new action.

All the succession plan's elements should be evaluated to uncover strengths and weaknesses. An observational report can be used to record the positives and areas for troubleshooting. The can also be used for making changes. Don't overuse these reports. This form of evaluation can turn minor problems into major ones if not properly supervised. It must not be the only means of your evaluation process.

DISCOVERING CAUSE AND EFFECT
(continued)

Regular succession planning meetings can also be used as a form of evaluation. These occasional check-ups can be used to monitor certain components of the program, such as:

- The plan's overall mission

- The plan's goals and objectives

- The methods for identifying talented employees

- Methods of appraisal

- Development activities and programs

- Stated key positions and requirements

The occasional check-up can keep the program in line with the company's objectives, which helps the succession plan succeed because problems will not develop from unaddressed operational changes.

To complete evaluation measures the program on all objectives and related activities. You will want to assess how the program is working in all of the areas of its design.

Use the following list as a guide for deciding what you will evaluate in your succession planning program. Check each item that now applies and make note to follow up on any that haven't been checked.

HOW ARE YOU DOING SO FAR? USE THE FOLLOWING CHECKLIST TO FIND OUT!

Does Your Program . . .

☐ Support the company's strategic objectives?

☐ Support individual career plans of potential executives?

☐ Support training efforts?

☐ Have a clear purpose?

☐ Have defined goals?

☐ Have measurable succession objectives?

☐ Have a way to identify talent?

☐ Have defined action steps for every phase?

☐ Have individuals responsible for it?

☐ Have a written succession policy?

☐ Have a commitment for all decision makers?

☐ Have incentives for mentors?

☐ Have an adequate development budget?

☐ Have a way to monitor results and keep records?

☐ Have a training plan for managers involved in the plan?

☐ Have a way to identify key positions?

☐ Have a way to identify future needs?

☐ Have a way to evaluate individual performance?

☐ Have a way to forecast position changes?

☐ Have a way to track all activities?

☐ Have a team to evaluate results?

USING THE RIGHT INSTRUMENT

Satisfaction Assessment

▶ Develop a survey that measures feelings about the program and its results.

▶ Ask questions about each area of the program.

Progress Made

▶ Use an instrument that will measure data and compare before and after individual movements.

▶ Ask mentors about progress.

Placements Completed

▶ Use a measurement instrument that provides quantitative data based on performance and analysis of each key position.

▶ Compare past completions to present activities.

Organizational Goals

▶ Use the plan to compare needs and the program's progress toward those objectives.

▶ Use projections to compare the program's perceived needs.

THE VALUE OF A COMPLETE ASSESSMENT

The complete assessment process takes the succession program evaluation one step further.

The process involves:

- ► A full system assessment using the program's criteria

- ► An abbreviated report using the program's criteria

- ► An assessment based on evaluation findings

The activities are valuable to the corporate succession plan because they:

- Involve and motivate succession participants

- Provide a proven evaluation system

- Focus on the company's goals

- Assess the commitment to every element of the program

- Provide hard, measurable data

- Provide feedback

- Encourage participation toward development

- Accelerate change toward its goals

- Improve ability to understand the workings of the program

- Provide a tool for continuous improvement

STAYING FOCUSED

In your final results, be sure to include all external environmental conditions that could have affected the program. The first few evaluations of the succession plan will be the most difficult; they will improve with practice and so will the program. The important things to remember are to stay committed to the program, to make adjustments where needed and to keep the program current with the company's needs. Don't take shortcuts in plan development, implementation or the evaluation process. Your efforts will pay off with solid leadership continuity.

Final Comments

A succession planning program is something that no company should be without. With changes happening almost daily, it is imperative that we prepare for the future. Knowing how to avert succession crises is a must. Plan not only for the continuation of your company, but the continuation of leadership. Take action by recognizing high potential employees. Develop successors in each employee group and provide opportunity. When you foster a climate for growth, you attract and retain employees who take responsibility and nurture success. Take stock of talent in your organization, for there is no greater motivator than having someone believe in you. When preparation meets opportunity, the possibilities are endless.

Good Luck!

Assessment

SYSTEMATIC SUCCESSION PLANNING

SYSTEMATIC SUCCESSION PLANNING
BUILDING LEADERSHIP FROM WITHIN

A FIFTY-MINUTE™ BOOK

The objectives of this book are:

1. to explain the benefits of a systematic succession plan.

2. to help you develop a succession program to meet your organization's needs.

3. to show how to identify leaders and leadership positions.

4. to explain the operation and evaluation of a systematic succession plan.

OBJECTIVE ASSESSMENT FOR SYSTEMATIC SUCCESSION PLANNING

Select the best answer.

1. Succession planning is used only for replacing employees after they have retired.
   A. True
   B. False

2. Many companies make the mistake of focusing only on management positions when developing their succession plan.
   A. True
   B. False

3. A true succession plan will provide
   A. development programs.
   B. defined goals and objective.
   C. a direction for corporate long-range planning.
   D. all of the above

4. A valuable reason to have a succession plan is to
   A. cut back on paper work.
   B. establish a pool of gifted employees to fill key positions.
   C. keep the work to a minimum.

5. Restructuring a company should never interfere with the employees and their work.
   A. True
   B. False

6. When developing your succession plan, you should
   A. identify high potentials.
   B. benchmark the practices of the best companies.
   C. analyze completely the jobs in your company.
   D. all of the above

7. In order to have a solid succession plan, you must first
   A. have a defined mission statement and clear purpose for the plan.
   B. get a cup of coffee.
   C. hire someone to do your job.

OBJECTIVE ASSESSMENT (continued)

8. If your company decides to take the corporate directed approach to the succession planning process, it would consider which of the following.
   A. using another plan of action to maintain a competitive edge.
   B. the visions and values of the executives.
   C. asking the customers for their opinion.

9. Succession planning and replacement planning are different.
   A. True
   B. False

10. You should not use a generic plan for your organization because every company will have different requirements and objectives.
    A. True
    B. False

11. Benchmarking companies that have exemplary succession plans in place can help you guide your program in order to meet your succession needs.
    A. True
    B. False

12. A succession plan policy statement is valuable only if it is
    A. long and detailed.
    B. clear, concise and in writing.
    C. kept in a safes.

13. Key leadership positions are always the top five executives in the company.
    A. True
    B. False

14. A highly competitive company often recruits for future needs before present duties are considered, but firsts they must
    A. identify future projects.
    B. identify the experts in the company.
    C. hire a recruiter.

15. When conducting a position analysis, you should
    A. outline position activities, individual responsibilities and team responsibilities.
    B. have a clear understanding of all job duties, functions, and activities.
    C. both of the above

16. Position descriptions need to be revised and updated periodically to meet the changing activities of the organization.
    A. True
    B. False

17. Exemplary performance can often be determined not only by the work accomplishments but also by having
    A. additional leadership qualities.
    B. a good sick leave record.
    C. an excellent assistant.

18. Performance appraisals differ from ordinary feedback and coaching because the appraisal
    A   requires advance preparation.
    B. is more detailed.
    C. follows an organized format.
    D. all of the above

19. Both environmental and external conditions can affect your organization's forecasting plan for job positioning.
    A. True
    B. False

20. When creating a climate for leaders, you must prepare for change with a vision of the future.
    A. True
    B. False

21. The only alternative to the traditional approach to filling positions is to distribute the work.
    A. True
    B. False

22. In order to provide proof that your succession plan is working, you must
    A. evaluate all dimensions of the plan.
    B. assess the cause and effect of any problems.
    C. communicate results.
    D. all of the above

OBJECTIVE ASSESSMENT (continued)

23. One efficient means for tracking your succession program's progress is to
    A. use professional computer software to track the program from the beginning.
    B. meet with all decision makers on a daily basis.
    C. hire people to help you.

24. Brainstorming sessions are a good way to make revisions that your program needs.
    A. True
    B. False

25. The following instrument should be used to help keep your succession assessment on track.
    A. satisfaction assessment
    B. progress data instrument
    C. quantitative-based instrument
    D. all of the above

Qualitative Objectives for *Systematic Succession Planning*

To explain the benefits of a systematic succession plan

Questions 1, 2, 3, 4, 5, 6

To help you develop a succession program to meet your organization's needs

Questions 7, 8, 9, 10, 11, 12

To show how to identify leaders and leadership positions

Questions 13, 14, 15, 16, 17, 18, 19, 20, 21

To explain the operation and evaluation of a systematic succession plan

Questions 22, 23, 24, 25

ANSWER KEY

1. B	10. A	18. D
2. A	11. A	19. A
3. D	12. B	20. A
4. B	13. B	21. B
5. B	14. A	22. D
6. D	15. C	23. A
7. A	16. A	24. A
8. B	17. A	25. D
9. A		

NOTES

NOTES

NOTES

NOW AVAILABLE FROM CRISP PUBLICATIONS

Books • Videos • CD Roms • Computer-Based Training Products

If you enjoyed this book, we have great news for you. There are over 200 books available in the *50-Minute*™ Series. To request a free full-line catalog, contact your local distributor or Crisp Publications, Inc., 1200 Hamilton Court, Menlo Park, CA 94025. Our toll-free number is 800-422-7477.

Subject Areas Include:

Management

Human Resources

Communication Skills

Personal Development

Marketing/Sales

Organizational Development

Customer Service/Quality

Computer Skills

Small Business and Entrepreneurship

Adult Literacy and Learning

Life Planning and Retirement

CRISP WORLDWIDE DISTRIBUTION

English language books are distributed worldwide. Major international distributors include:

ASIA/PACIFIC

Australia/New Zealand: In Learning, PO Box 1051 Springwood QLD, Brisbane, Australia 4127
Telephone: 7-3841-1061, Facsimile: 7-3841-1580   ATTN: Messrs. Gordon

Singapore: Graham Brash (Pvt) Ltd. 32, Gul Drive, Singapore 2262
Telphone: 65-861-1336, Facsimile: 65-861-4815   ATTN: Mr. Campbell

CANADA

Reid Publishing, Ltd., Box 69559-109 Thomas Street, Oakville,
Ontario Canada L6J 7R4.
Telephone: (905) 842-4428, Facsimile: (905) 842-9327   ATTN: Mr. Reid

Trade Book Stores: Raincoast Books, 8680 Cambie Street,
Vancouver, British Columbia, Canada V6P 6M9.
Telephone: (604) 323–7100, Facsimile: 604-323-2600   ATTN: Ms. Laidley

EUROPEAN UNION

England: Flex Training, Ltd. 9-15 Hitchin Street, Baldock,
Hertfordshire, SG7 6A, England
Telephone: 1-462-896000, Facsimile: 1-462-892417   ATTN: Mr. Willetts

INDIA

Multi-Media HRD, Pvt., Ltd., National House, Tulloch Road, Appolo Bunder,
Bombay, India 400-039
Telephone: 91-22-204-2281, Facsimile: 91-22-283-6478   ATTN: Messrs. Aggarwal

MIDDLE EAST

United Arab Emirates: Al-Mutanabbi Bookshop, PO Box 71946, Abu Dhabi
Telephone: 971-2-321-519, Facsimile: 971-2-317-706   ATTN: Mr. Salabbai

SOUTH AMERICA

Mexico: Grupo Editorial Iberoamerica, Serapio Rendon #125, Col. San Rafael,
06470 Mexico, D.F.
Telephone: 525-705-0585, Facsimile: 525-535-2009   ATTN: Señor Grepe

SOUTH AFRICA

Alternative Books, Unit A3 Sanlam Micro Industrial Park, Hammer Avenue
STRYDOM Park, Randburg, 2194 South Africa
Telephone: 2711 792 7730, Facsimile: 2711 792 7787   ATTN: Mr. de Haas